Praise for Refuge

"Jerome Gagnon's Refuge for Cranes plunge through a series of poems that are equal parts celebratory, revelatory, and prophetic. The poet reminds us of what poets are born to tell us—of the beauty of creation and of the paradox of its power and its fragility, the assurance that "everything changes into some other thing and this change goes on forever" and simultaneously of the troubling fact that "we've heard the whip crack of the flames and seen the horses running, scared, along the highway." Like the cranes that give the book its title, birds rumored to be immortal and wise, the poet bravely writes the truth he sees, "scratching our message to this passing world." Gagnon's poems enable the reader to live more intensely in the present moment and to glimpse the future, creating an intersection between worlds, actual and possible. Refuge for Cranes is a grace-filled book and a gift." — *Angela Alaimo O'Donnell, poet and author of Andalusian Hours and Holy Land*

*

"The unofficial yet consequential Anthropocene Epoch we find ourselves in seeps through these poems. Gagnon's curiosity and his attention to earthly things is vivid, but never overdone. At a jellyfish exhibit he asks "How would it be/ to live without bones, I wonder?/ Like smoke/ or an eerie flower without roots,/ but eyes that can see light/ and dark, tell up/ from down." There is a maturity and sense of scale in the distance (he selects an epigraph from Carl Sagan that urges us to preserve and cherish our pale blue dot of an earth) and close details of sleeping deer waking up, or bees poisoned with pesticide that "fly in circles close to the ground." Whether naming the generational consequences of war or a barking dog at a crosswalk that alerts us to the speeding pickup truck, Gagnon sustains a healthy tension in these poems. His first lines are casual and precise, signaling a running-start and giving us confidence that we'll be rewarded in some way by the end. We absolutely want to take in whatever things he will show us, which are, like the title of his beautiful poem on grief, "ordinary transformations." — *Katy Giebenhain, poet and author of Sharps Cabaret. Poems*

*

"If there was ever an offering of verse meant to be contemplation, it is Gagnon's Refuge for Cranes. I would be pressed to find a line in the book that did not hush my tongue and ask me to pause, so that I might pray-praise and hold the world holy. We are, in this poet's words, like "fawns on an early adventure / deep in the penultimate." How meaningful that word: the "penultimate". For we are near the end of a trail, not at the end; there is hope, but only just. An urgent stillness or a still urgency cores the moment. Watch with the "wisdom to leave things where they fall," the poet cautions. Let tenderness typify your touch. And thus, with the world, be." — *Sofia M. Starnes, poet and author of The Consequence of Moonlight*

*

"If you are looking for a beautiful, meditative journey that reveals the extraordinary through the ordinary, Jerome Gagnon's Refuge for Cranes is the book for you. 'You don't need to renounce anything,' he says, to encounter what 'flares up as happiness,' replenishing yourself and the world. Both thoughtful and prayerful, his poems lead the lucky reader through the open gate of his poetry into a greater appreciation of our world as it is, and as it could be." — *Julie Cadwallader Staub, poet and author of Wing Over Wing. Poems*

Refuge
for
Cranes

PRAISE POEMS
FROM THE
ANTHROPOCENE

Refuge
for
Cranes

Jerome Gagnon

Wildhouse
Poetry

for the two Annas
with love

CONTENTS

I

ORDINARY TRANSFORMATIONS

"The moment of change is the only poem."

—Adrienne Rich

When I Let Go

When I let go of the idea of getting it unalterably right,
the way things ought to be,
or of putting it all back together again,

when memory becomes a window into the lives
that have touched mine or, if not that,
a chance to apologize in the dark for errors of omission,

when I observe the spark of life in ordinary things,
the color of tangerines, say,
the way somebody has arranged them just so,

or overhear a child explain
that clouds are where birds sleep, never doubting it
for a moment—what more could I want?

Oleander Light

finds me looking for what it came from,
what it surrounds — morning floating in
and about the clustered flowers,

as if this was heaven's door or an opening
into something from the past,
a happiness forgotten —

leaves me lost in the sweetness
I wouldn't have thought to
put a name on.

Blue Jay Way

Most of what I know about them is hearsay,
that they're demons who prey upon the offspring
of songbirds. But that blue!
Flaming indigo in the pine, and within this,
the dark flash — beak that signals love or danger,
or both

              This morning,
I watched as a jay dropped
from a branch to the rim of a hollowed-out rock
filled with rainwater,
splashing blue under her wings, and then,
back to the branch —
       splash and branch, splash and branch.

I don't know how many times she made this journey
or how long I watched her lift from her spidery clasp,
each time landing on the edge of the unknown,
       head turning, warily, this way and that
before she entered the abyss, and —
           shivering —

flung epiphanies over the round stones
and tiny ears,
flowering in moss.

This Love of Earthly Things

1

It might be nothing more than wind
in the branches,
the gurgle of a spring creek,
bent grass in the morning, or something seen
out of the corner of your eye —
unidentified wings taking off in the distance.
Resting in the wayward moment,
in the way things are —
what could be more natural?

2

You don't have to renounce anything.
Just trust what's given: love and dissolution
under a blue umbrella sky,
fossil-embedded creeks
and carved ledges of Pleistocene,
dotted with ferns,
bursting pussy willows and cattails,
scent of cedar and pine,
icy wind against skin,
fur and claws, feathers and bones.

3

This love of earthly things will lift you
on snowy owl wings, and take you beyond
where the pine woods grow.
It will find you by a winter creek,
shorn of green and raven-wise,
and roam with you in the wilderness.
It will walk beside you on supple paws
and lie down next to you in the dark.

At a Jellyfish Exhibit

Most of them seem content to exist
in a half-dream, half-real state,
                              floating
in their tanks like tranquilized paratroopers
without a war
but still holding on to their parachutes
and, occasionally —
when the mood strikes —
                              lunging
toward the surface of the water,
as if they might suddenly leave their
bodies behind.

              And how would it be
to live without bones, I wonder?
Like smoke
or an eerie flower without roots,
but eyes that can see light
and dark, tell up
from down.

Early Poppies

They're everywhere now,
lifting through cracks in parking lots
and along the sides of roads,
orange petals closed to the chill
or flirting with the sun.

We used to see them around
the railroad tracks, tucked in the sparkle
of crushed granite that spilled down
from the tracks, and on the tracks themselves
where we went to put pennies on the rails,

to see what happened to them when a line of
boxcars passed by with a roar, warning us
what death must be like,
and then, tossed the ruined coins up
at the wires overhead, to hear them sing

as poppies do.

Begonia Days

We've driven down the coast to Capitola
in the green Chevy coupe with white wall tires
to see the begonias — my mother and father
in the front seat, my brother and I in back.

I'm ten years old,
walking among the striped shadows
made by the lathe work overhead,
eyeing the flowers arranged in rows on shelves
and dangling from clay pots above us.

I'm not sure what's to be seen in them, exactly.
Although they come in a variety of colors, the flowers
are sparse and the eel-like stems they sprout from
seem to have minds of their own,
as if they might slither out of their pots
and along the dark wooden planks
back to the sea.

The plants we bring back with us
blossom for two summers more
under the aluminum patio cover my father built
before we move on,
and now here in these random lines —

slow songs from a car radio somewhere along the coast,
afternoon glare of gravel in the parking lot
of the Shore Acres Motel,
the green neon sign flashing vacancy
off and on.

Walking Under Redwoods

It's the day before Christmas, what we call winter here:
ground still soggy from last week's rain, creeks running cold
but not so fast that a dog can't wade in for a ball
and stand there, stilled.
We've come for the scent of redwoods, seeking relief
from the relentless headlines that seem to spell doom
in capital letters and, as we walk, I listen
to my friend's travails and she listens to mine.

"I'm expendable," she says,
spitting out the word like an unripe catawba,
and I understand, completely — both of us survivors,
each in our way.
"Everything's changed," I say.
But what I'm really saying is that most everyone's gone,
most everyone I cared about —
as if they never were.

We've carried our stories with us into the woods,
knowing by heart their beginnings, their promises
and their endings,
spilling them beneath the tall canopy,
and I think to myself,
what are we here for, after all,
if not to immerse ourselves in this larger absence —
the silence among the trees?

Night Song

All around us, unseen birds
are preparing to roost,
finishing up their metallic songs
like so many innocuous toys.

The late shift will be coming on soon,
a party of one as far as I can tell —
the screech owl,
gone from the cypress for weeks now,
coming alive somewhere else.
Thank goodness for that.

When I first heard it I thought: *murder* —
not far off.
I can still hear it, screaming like a night train,
rails rattling,
stealing closer,
and then the ratcheting down,
only faster.

But mostly the hollow sound after.

Ordinary Transformations

1

Without warning, stones and petals,
lips and eyes, release their grip.
Boredom, too, dissipates like mist on a lake.
One by one my loves reappear, those who lifted me
and those who broke me,
each of them entering the longed-for realm,
shining, gone.

2

Do you suppose fire is only fire, cause and effect,
that it has a source or end in time?
Or that it burns within us, the dry tinder of need
waiting to erupt into undreamed of conflagrations?
White smoke rising in a white sky, becoming dust on
mustard leaves, sweat on a mule's back,
warmth of bread.

3

Long-smoldering, this grief gives off no light and little heat.
Lean into it though, and it flares up as happiness does,
etching its dazzling trail in the night sky.
Or else, it whiles its way to vacancy.
Like the skeleton of some once-quick rodent
found under a pile of leaves last fall,
it collapses in on itself —
shrouded, now, in morning glories.

Sleeping Deer in the Afternoon

I remember the sleeping deer as they awoke in the grass,
heads tilted to the scent of us —
seven or eight of them, one a fawn,
up and running through the old orchard,
                              flying across the creek,
disappeared in the brush.

                    White petals drifted by
like frail coins, as we moved
closer to where they'd lain —
bent green still warm.

I mourn the blackened trunks of the walnut trees;
my arms couldn't reach around them.
The orchard uprooted: hip-curve of hill
carved into lots;
                    where light dripped from branches,
the stare of gravel;
no more hum of bees, creek trickle.

I remember the deer, their flight as our breath held
and held —
trust they found another place to sleep
and pray no one comes across it.

Notes from Snow Mountain

After an easy climb, we found ourselves in the cone
of the dormant volcano.

It might have been a desert or an abandoned quarry —
all shards and gravel, foil for an unexpected pool,
not more than five feet deep and ten feet around,
like liquid topaz, like pale blue stationery
waiting to be written on.

I'd never seen anything so pristine,
without a ripple to disturb it, and wondered
who was there before us, who would come after?

It listened, warily, as we circled around it,
feet jostling stones as they slid down the banks
into water, what remained of winter's flurries,
what became of the old fury —

hidden river that burns within us, thick
and red.

*(Mt. Lassen, in California, was originally known as
Snow Mountain, or Kohm Yah-mah-nee in Maidu.)*

II

WHEN THE DAY BROKE
FIERY ORANGE

"If we could light up the room with pain,
we'd be such a glorious fire."

—Ada Limon

Of these three bowls —

the one for happiness, the one for dreams,
and the one for everything that goes wrong,
everything that might have been,

the first is filled with morning light
and random gestures,
a hand brushing a cheek, for one;

the second with a crow's bright findings,
crinkled tinsel, a red button,
a rusty bottle cap;

the third with loss and small trials:
I remember the spider I saw
climbing the walls of a porcelain sink,

the repeated, unheard fall,
the going on until —
thinking this is the strength of the frail

and the forgotten, persistence
of the spider goddess who spins the world
over and over again.

In the Cool of Morning

1
At dawn, we rise to the remains of a moon
shrouded in smoke,
news of a mass shooting in the capitol.
Drinking coffee, we contemplate the future,
swallowing our hearts.

2
Children in cages, separated from their mothers.
In the cities, the homeless sleep in cardboard boxes
and under freeway ramps, while the cunning invest in prisons.
Yet there's something that resists greed
and frees the oppressed — how do we grow that?

3
In the cool of morning, I sweep up bamboo leaves,
thinking of the poet Tu Fu who wrote about suffering
in a time of rebellion — 755 A.D., in China —
still pausing to observe willow twigs
sprouting at his gate.

When Bees Have Been Poisoned

—from an article in The Fresno Bee *(May 17, 2017)*

"They fly in circles close to the ground,"
or fall to the bottom of the hive in layers,
said apiarist Rafael Reynaga,
who lost dozens of hives in Reedley, Fresno County,
where they'd been placed to pollinate almond trees.

Because the bee corpses had traces of a pesticide
used on nectarines, scientists believe they were stricken
when visiting nearby nectarine orchards,
although reports indicate that recent spraying
appears to have been done according to regulations.

After the kill, Reynaga cleaned the hives with bleach
and relocated them, each with new broods and queens,
to a sanctuary in the foothills.
"I put them where they can thrive," he said.
"Now only time will tell."

Sites of the Shutdown

"A place must be made, still, for joy."
—Carl Phillips

These days it's hard to come by
where you might expect it, though you look for it
in the usual places — in the folds of ruffled roses,
in their perfume,

in the unscheduled appearance of an orange dragonfly,
the way the sun calls out to the drooping flowers
of the oleander at the end of the day,
how they shine on as they always do,

in the unripe peach you pick up from a bowl
on the kitchen table, the familiar warmth in your hand.
But none of these things move you
the way you want them to.

Where will you find it, then, if not here
in the stillest of places, in this empty house
splashed with summer's longing,
in this very room, this very body?

Invisible Ocean

—for my father

It's sometime around five a.m.
when I wake him for medicine and water.

Each sip has become a struggle
confounded by almost constant thirst.
Small sips, I say, to minimize choking.

How could I have forgotten how essential it is to swallow?
How we take the world in daily, an act as vital as breathing?

How the world will swallow us whole and expel us
into measurelessness?

How water receives water, a process so pervasive
it becomes almost invisible?

When the Day Broke Fiery Orange

The night before, we left the windows open
to air the house out, which was stifling from the heat —
109 degrees that day — and us with a portable air conditioner
that sounded like an airport runway at rush hour
and really didn't do all that much.

By morning it was clear that smoke from the fires up north
had drifted our way, lodging somewhere between
the floor of the world and the cloud cover above.
What light came through was like an orange cellophane wrapper
around a welcome basket.

You could barely breathe the air yet breathe it we did
for days afterward, although the orange glow eventually faded
to yellow and then to a smudgy gray that no longer evoked fears
of the apocalypse, but hope that shopping the farmer's market
or walking in the park might be doable before too much longer.

I don't know if Milton's vision of hell was meant as a metaphor
or a prophecy of what earth could become, is becoming —
whole towns swallowed in the night.
I don't know, except to say, we've heard the whip crack
of the flames and seen the horses running, scared,

along the highway.

Orpheus and the Animals

—after "Orpheus Charming the Animals," black ink and
brown wash on paper, by Josias Murer (about 1600)

The wild horses of the senses appeared at his side,
enamored by the songs he played on his lyre,
followed by a stubborn goat who lay agreeably
at his feet, and a murder of crows, hunched
in the branches of an olive tree.

Reptiles came, too, some on tiny lizard legs,
and then some unidentifiable swamp things came
which surely were from hell but, blessedly, fell
into a trance. And then the spotted deer arrived and
began to dance a magic circle dance.

At last, a leopard and an elephant came like visitors
from a dream, and stood together side by side:
"We're sparks of the sun and pieces of stars
and contain within us the animals and the elements," he sang.
So, hail all live things and all space!

Earthbytes

Perform your natural magic
like the bulb that emits the bloom.

Be in harmony with the brown bear,
the moon, and the music of reeds.

Restore the oceans and rivers,
the kelp forests, marshes and bays.

Repair the hives of bees
and the resting places of monarchs.

Embrace the other, brother and sister.
See no one and nothing as the enemy.

Notice this place as if for the first time
as if it was your own skin, your own bones —

draw strength here, and return it.

Viewing a Detail from Eighteen Songs of a Nomad Flute:
The Story of Lady Wenji

We suppose that the picturesque warriors on their mounts
were much the same as ours today,
not in their weapons or dress but their fervor,
and that their leaders were much the same as ours, too,
in their need for power, what passes as power.
That the wars men perpetrate on other men
are visited on the women and children of their enemies,
as much as on themselves.
That, even as these horrors go on in the name of righteousness,
there is some small, green corner of the heart
that yearns for peace and longs for beauty,
untouched by the terrible.

Lady Wenji says: "If you know the truth of this, speak out."

*(Artist and date unknown; Lady Wenji was kidnapped by a
warring chieftain during the Han Dynasty in China; years later
she was ransomed and allowed to return home, but without
her two children.)*

Elegy for Birds

*"Hundreds of thousands of migratory birds
have been found dead in New Mexico."*
—CNN, 9/14/20

Some species that are normally found ruffling in branches
have been seen, listless, on the ground,
while others fall around them or drop from the sky.
No one is exactly sure why.

In a wooded hollow, we heard the yellow warblers
singing for no reason other than the rain that fell
lightly from the branches,
causing them to raise and lower their wings
like animated flowers.

It may be that the dry weather and smoke from fires
damaged their lungs, while climate change
and the scarcity of insects are other factors cited in the die off,
which includes songbirds such as warblers, bluebirds,
flycatchers, and sparrows.

Bury them in newspaper scented with a tincture of herbs
and sprinkled with seeds.
Cover the place with leaves and branches,
and pieces of wind.

Once I saw a peregrine falcon charge down

twenty floors from its perch on a high-rise, and strike
a pigeon so hard that it died instantly in air
before the she-bird circled around to catch it
in its talons and carry it near the nest
where the hatchlings were —

and wouldn't change that —

but I'm still struck by the sight of dead bobcat
on the highway median last week,
lying there on its side for days
as the traffic passed by,
coming and going in a nowhere world.

III

REFUGE FOR CRANES

"Preserve and cherish the pale blue dot,
the only home we've ever known."
—Carl Sagan

Varieties of Peace

Like snow, it comes in myriad varieties
and often without notice.
Or it may be that peace is all there is.
I mean to say, it's there all the time,
almost unrecognized in its ordinariness
like early morning light,
the way a wall meets a door,
passing shadows over a ravine
or the music of bassoons in the trees.

We know what it's not, what's not cordial to it:
anger, as a rule, dishonesty,
pride and resentfulness — these go without saying —
self-pity, as well,
although each of these might serve
as an opening into something else,
something larger.
How everything changes into some other thing
and this change goes on forever.

Like snow on snow, it drifts down all around us
as we rise up to meet it on graphite branches
and the eaves of stranger's houses,
shaking it loose from our hair and shoes.

Driftwood

Not knowing that you would arrive in this house,
on this table, even less that you're a "you" —
chunk of redwood burl —

you set off down the flooded San Lorenzo River,
finding yourself on a sandbar, miles from home,
licking salt.

Not knowing yourself as an object of affection, either,
something to be stroked, polished with paste wax,
set on a high shelf, and then, years later,

in the back of a closet with boxes of photos
of the long-departed, sunning on blankets
and posed with cars —

paused, now, on a stack of books
like a small, curled wave,
the forgotten dreams pouring through.

Likening

Some days I wonder about the likening,
the way sycamore leaves confer
with light,
are enough like it to shine
and flicker, flicker
and darken;

how, in the morning, dense webs
are draped across the shaped evergreens
of dim front yards
like slivers of fog, hanging
from the hilltops and
lingering
in the crevasses;

how the fence post defers to the bouncing wren,
both of them weathered the same
dull brown, a canopy
for their joy —

everything connected,
everything a part of all that's around it.

And whenever I begin a poem likening one thing
to another, I have to wonder
if I've misspoken,
should have stayed quiet longer
like a motor
idling,
like
a
stranger
at the shrine.

November Turning

The secret of winter is contained in fall.
Cold cheeks, the brilliance of red camellias,
redder for the white flowers nearby.

The fig tree has withered — maybe next year, fruit.
Meanwhile, I've gotten out the extra blanket.
Neighbor's windows are closed tight.

Rain is coming, and nights with stars so bright
I'll think, again,
like seeing through the inside of a diamond.

Beauty, After

By which I mean the rose and the image of the rose,
the wood lark's song and Coltrane's deconstruction of it,
not to mention Buster P. as he rounds second, liquid,
river-ferocious,

by which I mean that which stays then vanishes —
you don't ask where it's gone,
you will have forgotten all about the varieties of purple,
falling over an unmended fence,

obsessed with this other thing, how it fashions meaning
from form and shadow,
while conceding a glass vase all rights to remain
empty on a wooden table.

What the Light Becomes

Some of it scatters like split ice
into a million pieces,
becoming the glint on bee wings
a rainbow slick on the road.

Some of it lands on the edges
of made things — tabletops and dressers,
buckles and keys,
and the crumbling book of lies.

Some of it seeps into the earth,
concocting antidotes for sorrow.

Some of it lives in the heart
as concentrated as the color blue
of corn flowers, as bright as the eyes
of the just-born and the very old.

Some of it enters the veins of trees
and rocks, calling on rain
to drench everything
in emptiness.

Some of it lives in stillness
and some of it flies like lightning
in the space between our bodies
when we touch.

Five Horses Running

This little brush and ink painting on newsprint,
found in the secondhand store,
is most likely meant to auger strength and success,
traditional themes.

I'm taken by the rendition of hooves and manes,
the way they so easily convey movement,
and by the long necks and tails,
charged with intent.

The accompanying poem, running vertically
in the left-hand margin, is a mystery,
although I think I decipher something in the ideograms —
spirit, eternity.

But much is missing.
Where do these horses come from
and where are they going?
All of them headed in the same direction,

galloping off the page
and onto the muddy plain of uncertainty,
where the tame scarcely venture
and the wild go, unseen.

Folding Handkerchiefs

My father's handkerchiefs are spotted with paint
like his jeans, the same beige paint he used
to paint the walls of the house after my mother died.

Light sifts through them as if they weren't even there
and, as I fold the warm cotton in quarters,
wonder if they long to return to the blazing fields

they came from, or if they're content to disperse
in shreds, corners curled like the fingers
that once lifted them easily from the drawer.

Morning Song

Forget for a moment the idea of an ending,
which isn't an ending.
How could it be when nothing ever ceases
to merge with the cosmic traffic?
You know, that crazy thing that stars do,
are forever doing, raining down
their fiery decrescendos,
white ink on black.

Didn't someone say the camel has another camel
inside of it?
Well, the blazing maple has another maple
inside of it, too, and another,
and each note of the yellow grosbeak's song
is a heralding of the infinite,
as if lithe fingers
were trilling the uttermost keys.

What's the wide-open secret inside of you,
the one word that echoes down through your days
and nights and years?
Let it ring out like a drunken bell across a valley,
holding in the trees,
so that it delights the small moths there,
freckled salmon in the streams,
the loving and unloving equally.

Irises Speak

We don't know why you planted us in rows
or what you see in us, exactly.
We're just happy to be alive
and to announce what's coming.

Yes, we've been told we're beautiful,
but we don't see it — isn't that always the way?
Think of photos of yourself when you were young
and leaning into the promise of womanhood —

you'd still find something to be critical of,
wouldn't you?
In the same way, we're immune to beauty,
although we're aware it draws tenderness to us

and an audience of dazed, winged things.
That's why we whisper at your arrival,
knowing you'll tell the truth about us —
that our real power isn't in effulgence

but our long abiding.

To the Keeper of Names

Notice the leaning creatures and things
animated by wind: every flower and person,
butterfly and stick, tells about itself, incessantly.

                              Be still
like the larger animals, listening
with ears big as the elephant's.

Collect the delicate pulse of friend's touch,
more valuable than ivory, kept in a transparent box.

Follow the alleys of any city you're in
to find the marvelous stairway.

                    Knock at the door
that resembles yours of a past hell.
Who lives there, now?

                        Celebrate —
dance, and indulge the spirit in a frenzy of prayer.

When you speak of loss, leave off the lessons:
                              be the monarch,
and the frost on the wings of the monarch.

                  Spell out things that have no name
if you're a keeper of names.

If you're as a sieve, air of words breathe in
and out of you,
                        into the mouths of others.

The Unseen

1
Everything depends on it — flower and seed,
form and no form, wheelbarrow
and the idea of a wheelbarrow,
the perennial question, "Why?"

2
Fog hangs over the hills this morning
like a sleepy apparition.
An unseen witness rejoices in the trees.
Why hurry to get where we're all going?

3
This tea is heaven-sent,
tended by calloused fingers.
Let me sit and savor it while the fog moves
deeper in the crevices.

Enquiry

How it rears its head in the most unexpected places,
minuscule wheels of yellow in the form of dandelions
growing around a trash can by the side of the road.

How it expands beyond the initial question —
"Why here?" to "Why not here?" —
to take in the cracked and gouged asphalt, too,
doing its job as best it can, given that it's motiveless.

How it comes to take in the gazer
along with passing traffic,
asking, "Who or what is it that's grateful?"
and finds what answers there are,
glinting among the detritus.

Cutting Back Morning Glory Vines Before a Storm

"Being and nonbeing are like vines clinging to a tree."
—Changqing Lan'an (793-883)

Here come the storm clouds and do I care?
Of course.
But they will have their darkening and their massing,
their vestiges of light in between,
their ominous conversation with everything
above and below for miles around.

Wearing my father's heavy jacket,
carrying clippers and a rake to trim back the rampant
morning glory vines, I begin pulling down the topmost layer
that's risen like a green archipelago —
here a mountain, there a valley — and all around
this ocean of clouds, thickening like the leaves of summer.

Apart from nonbeing or clinging to it as an invisible vine?
Neither one or the other, or both together.
Cutting the curled tangles a little at a time, I toss them in a pile.
A songbird has settled somewhere in the next yard.
"Changqing, Changqing," it sings, dispersing
the powdery notes of the sage's metaphor on the wind.

One True Face

The one true face delights in hiding itself
like a woman with an occult past
seeking her original happiness in the curve of a bowl,
call of a passing crow,
scent of dried grass in August.

That happiness is everywhere, isn't it? —
shining back onto the surface of the moon and sky
like still water —
an old sanctitude, deep in the well of us,
waiting to be drawn.

Refuge for Cranes

1
At dawn,
the Sandhill cranes descend on the flooded fields
in waves, with a clapping of wings
and a chain of trumpet calls.
To say they're like swollen reeds isn't it, they're like saplings
with wings, taller than the grape vines that grow
not far from here in what was once a vast slough.
To see them is to see parts of them, the pieced
carapace of their one life.

2
They stand in the shallows on stilt-like legs
contemplating stillness and any movement in stillness,
wings wrapped closely to their cores.
If they move at all, it's to stalk or bow
at the prospect of another morsel in the broth
which they firmly snatch in their beaks and swallow.

3
We won't see the likes of them again,
skimming the surface of the water,
their enormous wings combing the air.
A child could be carried by them, or an old soul
be transported to the moon —
our doubts dissolved in their lurching climb,
the piercing notes.

Things Are Opening Up Here, Again

Walking across the parking lot of our local mall
past a boarded up savings and loan,
I spotted dozens of fallen cones,
most of them about ten inches long,
at the base of an old pine tree.

The grounds hadn't been tended in over a year
is my guess, and the cones were an unexpected sight,
nestled in a bed of dried needles,
waiting for their chance to split open
and be tossed here and there.

I read once that German coal miners
found three pine cones embedded in rock
dating from 120 thousand to 15 million years,
and when put in water, the scales of the cones opened
slowly, but they opened.

What I saw scattered at my feet
was the patience I've dreamed of, the thing
that will outlive us if we let it, past the pandemic,
the rising waters and all the rest,
and I think so often it comes down to this —

recognition of the possible
and the wisdom to leave things where they fall.

Insects in Earthquake Weather

1
Something in the stare of a fly on the sill,
as if glued there, holds the world in place for a breath.
I wonder about this: if the fly's cycle of birth,
old age, suffering, and death is really the same as mine —
touched by the same grace and fear.

2
This moment is the arrival.
Worms are eating the *Treatise of Heaven and Earth*.
Am I dreaming or is this tortured place a garden?
I look under the banana palm leaf to find the queen of snails,
the delicate armor, the opalescent trail.
Where has she hidden?

3
In air, wings of the cabbage butterfly slow.
Wings meet like pilgrims hands, then soar, again,
into light.

Barking Dog

On days such as this,
if you happen to be walking in a crosswalk
and a speeding pickup jumps a red light,
a barking dog coming toward you
may cause you to change your course
just enough to save your life.

Can I just say that the gentle gust of displaced air
against your cheek as the truck speeds by
is the caress of death as it moves on to another city
and leave it at that?

Sometimes, light comes into our lives unannounced
like a speeding truck and a barking dog —
there isn't even time for the thought,
What could this possibly mean?

Three

1

The raspberries are plump
and the lake is a mirror of everything that ever was
and will be.
The frogs and the jumping fish know this.

2

To find a measure of happiness here is rare.
To know joy and sadness as one must be rarer still —
all of it a flowering, a fading and falling,
and this process going on again, and again.

3

At night, stars put on their ancient gowns
and spill nectar through the air.
In the morning the bees in the lavender, and we,
drink that nectar.

Night and Day

Let me welcome the dark, too,
and what lives in the dark —

stars, for one,
and the small fires here below
between lovers and others;

fireflies, of course,
those who run to catch them
and those who let them go;

dreams of the imprisoned
and the embers
of our nearly forgotten losses.

Let me welcome the night,
stripped of shadows
and familiar stories,

feeling along this blanket of sighs,
gliding low over rooftops
before the light reinvents us.

Fig Tree

I could swear this tree is the center of the universe,
springing forth with hundreds of hands,
each of them bearing figs, dark and musky
in the valley's fading light.

Surely three is enough, so sweet, so juicy.
But no.
Even the rats in the palm aren't as greedy.

Have I ever been this ripe with desire and delight?
And who could begin to tell one from the other?

For Once

For once, the sound of a train passing by doesn't remind me
of days past, two short whistles and then nothing,
and the green flash of a hummingbird doesn't suggest
the transience of things, as if that was its intention —
but I don't think of that as I watch it make its rounds
among the plumbago flowers, a process that isn't much
like the mind flitting from thought to thought either,
although you hear about that sort of thing often enough,
and in case you may be wondering where all this is leading,
I should add that the old aluminum timer that sits on a shelf
by the oven doesn't come close to evoking the mystery
of a heartbeat or even, with its metallic insistence, a train
hurling itself forward and then, circling back
to the immensity between the lines.

Eye of the Heart

1
Say you draw a circle around yourself
and walk freely there, surrounded by love.
Say you expand this circle, farther than you've ever been.

2
The way a seed fulfills itself and fallen things
replenish the world — here, now, the ends of branches
are bright with berries and ripe for the feasting of blackbirds.

3
May you find yourself in a clearing after a light rain.
May you enter a spacious house and be welcomed at the table.
May all your troubles vanish.

Day of the Long Night Moon

1

The moon is low in the north this morning
as the sun rises and frost drips from the rooftops.
Wisdom is near in the glow of leaves
and forgiveness in the mud.

2

Trying to hold onto this brightness is useless,
like carrying silver coins in a pocket full of holes.

3

Not knowing what trials may come, knowing only
that she's always beside me as I step in and out
of the river of doubt, I think:
"Who would guess that this slow moon is also
the giver of gifts, mother of wonder?"

IV

ENCOMIUM FOR A
GARDEN

"That night, in my bed, when I closed my eyes,
bee hum ran through my body."
—Sue Monk Kidd

Ars Poetica

There isn't only the blank page, although there's that,
and the unmeasured notes you scrawl across it.
And then, if you bear down into the crux
where the meanings are, they may break apart

in the sleeping bell of your heart,
which is where music occurs, isn't it?
Not the why of olives on the branch,
new as baby's toes, but their unexpected caroling.

Sometimes, you may not necessarily have made
an image of a tree, say, or a dog.
Or, if you have, they don't simply resemble
but murmur, bark.

The more difficult subjects — love, grief,
the transparency of grace —
may sleep for years before they awaken
as light weeping through honey,

as a bluejay's call, slipping
though cobwebs.

Insomnia

It's late, maybe later than I think,
but before I go back to bed, peek out of the shutters
at the little, weeping pear tree, dressed in white
and aglow from the porch light next door.

Why do I need to write this down?
That the fallen petals lie around it in a bright penumbra
or that this moment between waking and sleeping
is worthy, steeped in silence?

I can't think when it's ever been so pervasive,
able to hold a multitude of voices
in its dark throat, my own in particular, struggling
not to utter the words that keep me from sleep.

December Gate

Everything soaked from last night's storm,
rich with the scent of leaf-life and soil-dank,
and just as I suspect, the rain barrel is about to overflow,
a crimson petal floating on the surface of the water.

Something clogging the spout
at the bottom of the barrel, or it might be
a dead mouse in the hose as it was another year —
and as I begin bailing water out with a leaky plastic bin,
feel the drizzle start up again,
keeping time with my dipping in and out,
or am I keeping time with the rainfall
as I toss water several feet from the house
as far as I can?

Spray of water on morning glory vines and rose stubble,
a pregnant caesura in-between,
bearing me into something like happiness.

I thank this place for its dark and green-damp,
for all that tumbled down in the night,
for what's grown up through the cracks in planks
and climbed across the wall,
for the cold water spilling from my hands
and the open gate, most of all.

When It Appears

When it appears between the curtains,
under the drawn shade,
touching everything with possibility,
illuminating the dim corners of your room,
the keys and spare change spread across the dresser
and the clothes you hung over the chair last night —
know that its name is yours,
that you hold it in the palm of your hand
like a small, warm bird
that you release with each breath,
so that it may deliver its message to others
who are waiting for something like hope,
something like song.

Opening of the Pier

For a moment he seemed more than a boy,
part bird, part myth,
            flung into the air
from a diving board on an old pier —

arms raised and outstretched,
lower legs tucked up behind him —
and in that moment he soared out of time,
not of earth but sky

until the surface of the water claimed him
and took him down
past adolescence, onto the fields of war
and love.

But in that moment he left behind all
he had been and, uncertain of the future,
flew without wings as long and as high
as it was possible for a boy,

and as we watched from our places in line,
I think each of us must have imagined
how it would feel, again,
to live as if joy was everything.

Encomium for a Garden

Knowing this could never be an escape like drink
or even a hobby,
but taking as my model the bees, their one-pointedness,
I set about minding the light and shadow of the place,

gradually acquiring some basic tools of the trade,
squirreling them away where I'd most likely need them —
a trowel here, a glove there —
finding solace in my haphazard devotions.

To what?

Not beauty, per se, or the feel of the soil,
or even the fleet radiance of a hummingbird,
but the soul's deep down unfathoming,
this loosening and coming undone,

watching roses go to pot and beds to seed,
fluff of dandelion drifting downwind in autumn —
and all the while the bees, dinning in my ears
their one, persistent song of praise.

Sumi-e

Those things the old painters set down
speak to us still: the willingness of bamboo
to embrace wind comes to mind;

bursting cattails in fall;

the way a glint of irises defers to rock;

how freedom is like a kite
leading us beyond the frame —

how the non-doing of a painter's brush
can bring us face to face with a pond snail

and other wonders we may have missed
in our mad rush to oblivion.

Lines Written on an Envelope

1
The pen in my hand moves like a dowser's rod
seeking water, not apart from water.
The hand sings, the heart releases.
A spring of seasons erupts: leaves blossoming
in autumn, a child's eyes on the face of a stone,
growing into the shape of an old man,
uttering prayers, tending embers.

2
Every rock and tree,
all the animals and insects,
every shell, cloud, and wildflower,
stars, planets, time, light, and breath
arise from and are sustained by this mystery.
Eyes closed, this not-seeing is that;
open it's that, too.

3
What is the poem?
Steam returning to air,
ice and ashes,
evidence of passage, passing,
a song for my parents, not yet born.

Why You Should/Should Not Plant Morning Glories

It's true, I'm a fool to plant morning glories
anywhere near roses, or to plant the former at all.
Now, here I am this morning in a soup-stained sweater,
cutting a path through a carpet of them
designed to trip me up — and they almost do.

                              Climbing down
from a retaining wall hidden in vines,
I spot a newly opened red rose next to a purple flower
as if posed for a family portrait —
staring out at this follower of buds, mostly unbroken.

Land's End

Through light-strewn branches we go,
aware of unexpected pleasures:

the glistening of spring's familiar weeds,
bending underfoot;

banana slug crawling on a leaf;

small birds flitting in and out of the branches;

the ground itself, barely visible
for the young life everywhere.

The trail is nearly unfound.

On it leads us like fawns on an early adventure,
deep in the penultimate.

Fire on Water

Beams of August sunlight,
sparking the surface of the pond.

Who are they trying to delight?

Not the clouds, luminescent;
something deeper down.

A spectral stone has lived there
since before trees.

It gathers heat from below,
memories of falling stars,

stews in its murky lair until ready,
and is sent up to the surface.

And some will say,
Here is fire burning on water,

and others will say, *Here is fire
dancing in the heart-stone.*

For the purveyor of small things

who puts the burr in my shoe
and the hum in bees,

who brings from the river-fall its bubbles
and cultivates the rosemary flower,

giver of crumbs to the mouse,
confidant of ants, gnats, and fleas,

keeper of gemstones and wax wings,
of buttons, thimbles,

and broken bits —
praise for the purveyor of small things

in which greatness lives as a seed,
and each one fits among the others.

A Charm of Finches

All winter long, I moved like a sleepwalker
through the low-hanging fog and rainy days of the lockdown.
Now that spring is here I don't know what to do with myself.

From the window I track a hummingbird from bush to bush,
then head out back to pick up the plumbago
and morning glory vines I cut down yesterday, filling three bins.

Suddenly, the rosemary bush is aflame
with yellow-green finches, feeding on purple blossoms
and performing their aerial acrobatics as if for an audience of one,

and if for every loss there's a resurrection,
a charm of finches, or whatever,
then bring them on, bring them on.

Meditation without an Object

The ashes of the past have blown here and there
like blackened butterfly wings.
A thousand poems won't fill that spaciousness,
or a lifetime of lovers' sighs.
This brittle form, too, will perish
and what will remain then?

Meeting in the Field

If sorrow is the salt of life as my grocer says,
his smile bright enough to light the world,
then what is our joy?

Something like kindness, I think,
the best we give of ourselves when we enter
the green field of the other.

Knowing the likenesses of these —
the salty and sweet, the one in the other —
may be the closest I can come to wisdom.

And maybe that's what the golden-breasted one
has been getting at, after all,
perched on the telephone wire this evening,

singing a sweet song shot through with pain,
singing a wise song for all who'll listen,
for everything, really, that lives under the sun.

Walking in Snow

Like the mule deer that sheds its antlers,
I've left behind the old parts of my life,
walking with a lighter step in snow,

uncertain why I've come here,
if not for this cluster of mushrooms
at the base of a powdered fir,

the sight of my breath in the cold air,
and glad for it.

We, Cranes

We've gone gray here
in flat river, fleshing out the muskeg
around icy bogs,

purring and pointing our beaks
to the sun, we call to the everything
and the one.

We're in our center,
a sworl of wings and chortles,
                              rising up

like stink from a sandbar,
                              gliding,
dancing, stalking,

bowing,
scratching our message
to this passing world.

Saving Cranes

Among the organizations dedicated to saving cranes, their habitats, ecosystems, waterways, and flyways:

Save Our Sandhill Cranes (SOS Cranes), in partnership with the Sacramento Audubon Society, is dedicated to the preservation of California Central Valley's Sandhill Crane population and their habitats. They conduct free tours between October and March. www.soscranes.org

The International Crane Foundation (ICF) was founded in 1973 by Cornell students Ron Sauey and George Archibald on a horse farm in Baraboo, Wisconsin. Combining research, breeding, landscape preservation, and education, the work of the organization now reaches worldwide. www.savingcranes.org

The Woodbridge Ecological Reserve (variously known as the Isenberg Crane Reserve) is located in Lodi, California. This 353-acre reserve provides a freshwater wintering site for Greater and Lesser Sandhill Cranes, the largest in the state, as well as for tundra swans, snow geese, pheasant, and small songbirds. Docent-led tours are available. www.wildlife.ca.gov

The Nature Conservancy acquired Staten Island in San Joaquin Valley, a 500-acre wintering site for Sandhill Cranes, in 2001, to support conservation and protect their habitats from development. www.nature.org

The Bosque Apache National Wildlife Refuge in San Antonio, New Mexico, is the wintering site for thousands of Sandhill Cranes who arrive in late October each year. Audubon New Mexico and Arizona have recently joined together as Audubon Southwest to conserve habitats along the Rio Grande that cranes and other bird species depend on. www.nm.audubon.org

Acknowledgments

My thanks to the following magazines and sites where the poems listed below previously appeared:

"Beauty, After": *Linden Avenue Journal*

"Blue Jay Way": *Pinyon*

"Driftwood": *Third Wednesday*

"Eighteen Songs of a Nomad Flute: The Story of Lady Wenji": *Poems, for Now, River Heron Review*

"Encomium for a Garden": *Spiritus*

"In the Cool of the Morning": Honorable Mention, Barbara Mandigo Kelly Poetry Peace Prize Contest (2020)

"Invisible Ocean": *The Healing Muse, a Journal of Literary and Visual Art*

"Meeting in the Field": "The Origami Poems Project" in *The Best of Kindness Anthology, 2017*

"Night Song": Loon Magic and Other Night Sounds, Grand Prize in the *TallGrass Writers Anthology*

"Notes from Snow Mountain": *Humana Obscura*

"November Turning": *Dodging the Rain*

"Oleander Light": *Ocotillo Review*

"Ordinary Transformations": *Passager*

"Sites of the Shutdown": *Pensive: A Global Journal of Spirituality and the Arts*

"Sleeping Deer in the Afternoon": *Canary*

"Things are Opening Up Here, Again": *Passager*

"To the Keeper of Names": *Occam's Razor*

"Varieties of Peace": *Crosswinds*

"Walking Under Redwoods": *California Quarterly*

"When It Appears": *Spiritus 19*

This book is set in Optima typeface, developed by the German type-designer and calligrapher Hermann Zapf. Its inspiration came during Zapf's first trip to Italy in 1950. While in Florence he visited the cemetery of the Basilica di Santa Croce and was immediately taken by the design of the lettering found on the old tombstones there. He quickly sketched an early draft of the design on a 1000 lira banknote, and after returning to Frankfurt devoted himself to its development. It was first released as Optima by the D. Stempel AG foundry in 1958 and shortly thereafter by Mergenthaler in the United States. Inspired by classical Roman inscriptions and distinguished by its flared terminals, this typeface is prized for its curves and straights which vary minutely in thickness, providing a graceful and clear impression to the eye.